QUADRILLE

ONE SENT-ENCE A DAY

A MEANINGFULNESS JOURNAL

mean-ing-ful-ness

full of meaning, significance, purpose, or value linking the past, present and future

START HERE

MY NAME IS:

- -

**IN CASE OF LOSS, THEFT OR ANY
OTHER ACCIDENT, PLEASE RETURN TO:**

....

....

....

**THE THING/OBJECT/PERSON
THAT MEANS THE MOST TO ME:** ....

....

THE BEST FILM/SONG/BOOK:

....

....

MY FAVOURITE PLACE IN THE WORLD:

....

**MY LAST 3 COURSES
ON EARTH WOULD BE:**

STARTER

MAIN COURSE

DESSERT

MY MOST REOCCURRING DREAM:

....

THE MOST INSPIRING QUOTE:

....

MY MOST MEMORABLE MOMENT:

....

WHAT DO I MOST WANT TO ACHIEVE:

....

INTRODUCTION

ONE SENTENCE A DAY IS A JOURNAL DESIGNED TO ADD MORE MEANINGFULNESS INTO YOUR LIFE.

Every day write down the most meaningful thing that happens to you. This practice will allow you to uncover which people, moments and experiences make your life more meaningful and it will also chart the evolution of exactly what makes you happiest throughout the year.

What today seems like an ordinary moment becomes much more special when you re-read it. By looking back at your sentences you will rediscover your past, find happiness in your present and explore how you could add more meaning into your future.

Re-reading your sentences and selecting your favourite memories will give you a better sense of yourself. You will begin to discover that it's not the extraordinary events that shape and form your life, it's the every day moments that give real meaning to it.

A meaningful life guides our actions from the past through the present and into the future – giving us a sense of the direction our lives should take. The sentences you write down in your journal will become a key to discovering exactly what will make your life more meaningful.

INSTRUCTIONS

Write down one sentence a day of the most meaningful thing that happens to you:

It could be a song lyric, an image, a piece of news, something you have eaten, a quote you have read, a compliment someone has given you, a happy thought, a good thing you have done for another person, a conversation you felt stimulated by, an emotion you strongly felt, a personal achievement or a discovery you have made.

However big or small, just recollect one thing that has meant the most that day. Jot down the date so you can later explore the entire course of your meaningful journey.

- When you reach a page that asks you to look back over your journal and select your favourite memories, spend a few moments reading through the sentences you have written and find the ones which most stand out.

- When you reach a page that asks you to write down or doodle a specific emotion, achievement, adventure or moment, re-read your journal and recall which of the experiences most stand out.

- When you have completed the journal and coloured in your map, cut off the cover and re-read every sentence.

It will now be your personal meaningfulness journal.

THE MOST MEANINGFUL THING THAT HAPPENED TODAY...

DAY ......

DAY ......

DAY ......

DAY ......

THE MOST MEANINGFUL THING THAT HAPPENED TODAY...

DAY ......

DAY ......

DAY ......

DAY ......

THE MOST MEANINGFUL THING THAT HAPPENED TODAY...

DAY _____

_____

_____

_____

_____

DAY _____

_____

_____

_____

_____

DAY _____

_____

_____

_____

_____

DAY _____

_____

_____

_____

_____

The most
meaningful
thing that
happened today...

Day ⎯⎯⎯

Day _____

Day _____

Day _____

TOP 10 THINGS THAT MAKE ME HAPPIEST

1

2

3

4

5

6

7

8

9

10

THE MOST MEANINGFUL THING THAT HAPPENED TODAY...

DAY ....

DAY ....

DAY ....

DAY ....

THE MOST MEANINGFUL THING THAT HAPPENED TODAY...

DAY _____

_____

_____

_____

_____

DAY _____

_____

_____

_____

_____

DAY _____

_____

_____

_____

_____

DAY _____

_____

_____

_____

_____

THE MOST MEANINGFUL THING THAT HAPPENED TODAY...

DAY ......

DAY ......

DAY ......

DAY ......

THE MOST MEANINGFUL THING THAT HAPPENED TODAY...

DAY ......

DAY ......

DAY ......

DAY ......

THE MOST MEANINGFUL THING THAT HAPPENED TODAY...

DAY___

DAY ___

DAY ___

DAY ___

TOP 5 THINGS I'VE DONE RECENTLY

1

2

3

4

5

The most meaningful thing that happened today...

Day ....

Day ....

Day | ....

Day | ....

THE MOST MEANINGFUL THING THAT HAPPENED TODAY...

DAY ......

DAY ......

DAY ......

DAY ......

THE MOST MEANINGFUL THING THAT HAPPENED TODAY...

DAY___

DAY ___

DAY ___

DAY ___

THE MOST MEANINGFUL THING THAT HAPPENED TODAY...

DAY ......

DAY ......

DAY ......

DAY ......

The most
meaningful
thing that
happened today...

Day ____ ....

....

....

....

Day ____

Day ____

Day ____

THE LAST
TRIP I TOOK

WHERE:

DOODLE IT/STICK THINGS IN I FOUND:

THE MOST MEANINGFUL THING THAT HAPPENED TODAY...

DAY ....

DAY ....

DAY ....

DAY ....

THE MOST MEANINGFUL THING THAT HAPPENED TODAY...

DAY ......

DAY ......

DAY ......

DAY ......

The most
meaningful
thing that
happened today...

Day _____

Day _____

Day _____

Day _____

THE MOST MEANINGFUL THING THAT HAPPENED TODAY...

DAY _____

_____

_____

_____

_____

DAY _____

_____

_____

_____

_____

DAY _____

_____

_____

_____

_____

DAY _____

_____

_____

_____

_____

THE MOST MEANINGFUL THING THAT HAPPENED TODAY...

DAY ......

DAY ......

DAY ......

DAY ......

**LOOK BACK OVER
THE PREVIOUS PAGES**

MY TOP 5
SENTENCES

1

2

3

4

5

The most meaningful thing that happened today...

Day ....

Day ....

Day ....

Day ....

THE MOST MEANINGFUL THING THAT HAPPENED TODAY...

DAY ......

DAY ......

DAY ......

DAY ......

THE MOST MEANINGFUL THING THAT HAPPENED TODAY...

DAY___

DAY___

DAY___

DAY___

THE MOST MEANINGFUL THING THAT HAPPENED TODAY...

DAY ......

DAY ......

DAY ......

DAY ......

THE MOST MEANINGFUL THING THAT HAPPENED TODAY...

DAY ....

DAY ....

DAY ....

DAY ....

What I have most looked
forward to today...

What I have most looked
forward to this month...

What I have most looked forward to this year...

THE MOST MEANINGFUL THING THAT HAPPENED TODAY...

DAY ......

DAY ......

DAY ......

DAY ......

THE MOST MEANINGFUL THING THAT HAPPENED TODAY...

DAY _____

_____

_____

_____

_____

DAY _____

_____

_____

_____

_____

DAY _____

_____

_____

_____

_____

DAY _____

_____

_____

_____

_____

The most
meaningful
thing that
happened today...

Day_____

Day _____

Day _____

Day _____

THE MOST MEANINGFUL THING THAT HAPPENED TODAY...

DAY ......

DAY ......

DAY ......

DAY ......

The most meaningful thing that happened today...

Day ....

Day ....

Day | ....

Day | ....

THE LAST THING I HEARD, READ OR SAW THAT INSPIRED ME

DOODLE IT/ STICK IT IN HERE:

THE MOST MEANINGFUL THING THAT HAPPENED TODAY...

DAY___

DAY ___

DAY ___

DAY ___

THE MOST MEANINGFUL THING THAT HAPPENED TODAY...

DAY ......

DAY ......

DAY ......

DAY ......

The most meaningful thing that happened today ...

Day ....

Day ....

Day | ....

Day | ....

THE MOST MEANINGFUL THING THAT HAPPENED TODAY...

DAY ......

DAY ......

DAY ......

DAY ......

The most meaningful thing that happened today ...

Day ____ ....

....

....

....

Day _____

Day _____

Day _____

WHAT AM I PROUDEST OF...

HOW DID I ACHIEVE IT...

WHAT DOES IT MEAN TO ME...

THE MOST MEANINGFUL THING THAT HAPPENED TODAY...

DAY ....

DAY ....

DAY ....

DAY ....

THE MOST MEANINGFUL THING THAT HAPPENED TODAY...

DAY _____

_____

_____

_____

_____

DAY _____

_____

_____

_____

_____

DAY _____

_____

_____

_____

_____

DAY _____

_____

_____

_____

_____

THE MOST MEANINGFUL THING THAT HAPPENED TODAY...

DAY___

DAY ___

DAY ___

DAY ___

THE MOST MEANINGFUL THING THAT HAPPENED TODAY...

DAY ......

DAY ......

DAY ......

DAY ......

The most meaningful thing that happened today...

Day ....

Day ....

Day | ....

Day | ....

MY MOST MEMORABLE DREAM

....

....

....

....

....

....

....

....

....

....

....

....

....

....

....

....

....

....

DOODLE IT:

THE MOST MEANINGFUL THING THAT HAPPENED TODAY...

DAY ......

DAY ......

DAY ......

DAY ......

THE MOST MEANINGFUL THING THAT HAPPENED TODAY...

DAY ......

DAY ......

DAY ......

DAY ......

The most meaningful thing that happened today...

Day ....

Day ....

Day | ....

Day | ....

THE MOST MEANINGFUL THING THAT HAPPENED TODAY...

DAY ......

DAY ......

DAY ......

DAY ......

THE MOST MEANINGFUL THING THAT HAPPENED TODAY...

DAY___

DAY ___

DAY ___

DAY ___

THE MOST INTERESTING CONVERSATION I HAVE HAD RECENTLY

_____

_____

_____

_____

_____

_____

_____

_____

The most meaningful thing that happened today...

Day ....

Day ....

Day ....

Day ....

THE MOST MEANINGFUL THING THAT HAPPENED TODAY...

DAY ......

DAY ......

DAY ......

DAY ......

THE MOST MEANINGFUL THING THAT HAPPENED TODAY...

DAY ......

DAY ......

DAY ......

DAY ......

THE MOST MEANINGFUL THING THAT HAPPENED TODAY...

DAY _____

_____

_____

_____

_____

DAY _____

_____

_____

_____

_____

DAY _____

_____

_____

_____

_____

DAY _____

_____

_____

_____

_____

The most
meaningful
thing that
happened today...

Day _____

Day _____

Day _____

Day _____

LOOK BACK OVER
THE PREVIOUS PAGES
MY TOP 5
SENTENCES

1

2

3

4

5

THE MOST MEANINGFUL THING THAT HAPPENED TODAY...

DAY___

DAY___

DAY___

DAY___

THE MOST MEANINGFUL THING THAT HAPPENED TODAY...

DAY ......

DAY ......

DAY ......

DAY ......

The most meaningful thing that happened today...

Day ....

Day ....

Day | ....

Day | ....

THE MOST MEANINGFUL THING THAT HAPPENED TODAY...

DAY ......

DAY ......

DAY ......

DAY ......

THE MOST MEANINGFUL THING THAT HAPPENED TODAY...

DAY___

DAY___

DAY___

DAY___

LOOK BACK OVER
THE PREVIOUS PAGES
WHAT HAS
BEEN MY
FAVOURITE DAY

DOODLE IT/
STICK IT IN:

THE MOST MEANINGFUL THING THAT HAPPENED TODAY...

DAY ......

DAY ......

DAY ......

DAY ......

THE MOST MEANINGFUL THING THAT HAPPENED TODAY...

DAY _____

_____

_____

_____

_____

DAY _____

_____

_____

_____

_____

DAY _____

_____

_____

_____

_____

DAY _____

_____

_____

_____

_____

The most meaningful thing that happened today...

Day _____

Day _____

Day _____

Day _____

THE MOST MEANINGFUL THING THAT HAPPENED TODAY...

DAY ......

DAY ......

DAY ......

DAY ......

The most meaningful thing that happened today...

Day ....

Day ....

Day | ....

Day | ....

THE LAST TIME I LAUGHED...

THE LAST TIME I CRIED...

THE LAST TIME I FELT ECSTATIC...

THE LAST TIME I WAS ANGRY...

THE MOST MEANINGFUL THING THAT HAPPENED TODAY...

DAY___

DAY ___

DAY ___

DAY ___

THE MOST MEANINGFUL THING THAT HAPPENED TODAY...

DAY _____

_____

_____

_____

_____

DAY _____

_____

_____

_____

_____

DAY _____

_____

_____

_____

_____

DAY _____

_____

_____

_____

_____

THE MOST MEANINGFUL THING THAT HAPPENED TODAY...

DAY ....

DAY ....

DAY ....

DAY ....

THE MOST MEANINGFUL THING THAT HAPPENED TODAY...

DAY ......

DAY ......

DAY ......

DAY ......

THE MOST MEANINGFUL THING THAT HAPPENED TODAY...

DAY___

DAY___

DAY___

DAY___

WHO I WANT TO SEE MORE...

WHERE I WANT TO GO...

WHAT I WANT TO DO
MORE IN MY LIFE...

The most meaningful thing that happened today...

Day ....

Day ....

Day ....

Day ....

THE MOST MEANINGFUL THING THAT HAPPENED TODAY...

DAY _____

_____

_____

_____

_____

DAY _____

_____

_____

_____

_____

DAY _____

_____

_____

_____

_____

DAY _____

_____

_____

_____

_____

THE MOST MEANINGFUL THING THAT HAPPENED TODAY...

DAY ......

DAY ......

DAY ......

DAY ......

THE MOST MEANINGFUL THING THAT HAPPENED TODAY...

DAY ......

DAY ......

DAY ......

DAY ......

The most
meaningful
thing that
happened today...

Day____

Day _____

Day _____

Day _____

TOP 10 THINGS I WANT TO DO BUT HAVEN'T YET

1 ....

2 ....

3 ....

4 ....

5

6

7

8

9

10

THE MOST MEANINGFUL THING THAT HAPPENED TODAY...

DAY___

DAY ___

DAY ___

DAY ___

THE MOST MEANINGFUL THING THAT HAPPENED TODAY...

DAY ......

DAY ......

DAY ......

DAY ......

The most meaningful thing that happened today...

Day ....

Day ....

Day ....

Day ....

THE MOST MEANINGFUL THING THAT HAPPENED TODAY...

DAY _____

_____

_____

_____

_____

DAY _____

_____

_____

_____

_____

DAY _____

_____

_____

_____

_____

DAY _____

_____

_____

_____

_____

The most
meaningful
thing that
happened today...

Day ____

Day _____

Day _____

Day _____

WHAT CURRENTLY FILLS MY BOOKSHELF

A DOODLE OF MY BOOKSHELF:

THE MOST MEANINGFUL THING THAT HAPPENED TODAY...

DAY___

DAY ___

DAY ___

DAY ___

THE MOST MEANINGFUL THING THAT HAPPENED TODAY...

DAY ......

DAY ......

DAY ......

DAY ......

THE MOST MEANINGFUL THING THAT HAPPENED TODAY...

DAY ....

DAY ....

DAY ....

DAY ....

THE MOST MEANINGFUL THING THAT HAPPENED TODAY...

DAY ......

DAY ......

DAY ......

DAY ......

The most meaningful
thing that happened
today...

Day ....

Day ....

Day | ....

Day | ....

**LOOK BACK OVER
THE LAST PAGES**

TOP 5 PLACES
I HAVE VISITED

1

2

3

4

5

THE MOST MEANINGFUL THING THAT HAPPENED TODAY...

DAY ......

DAY ......

DAY ......

DAY ......

THE MOST MEANINGFUL THING THAT HAPPENED TODAY...

DAY _____

_____

_____

_____

_____

DAY _____

_____

_____

_____

_____

DAY _____

_____

_____

_____

_____

DAY _____

_____

_____

_____

_____

THE MOST MEANINGFUL THING THAT HAPPENED TODAY...

DAY ....

DAY ....

DAY ....

DAY ....

THE MOST MEANINGFUL THING THAT HAPPENED TODAY...

DAY ......

DAY ......

DAY ......

DAY ......

The most meaningful thing that happened today...

Day ___

Day ____

Day ____

Day ____

TOP 10 THINGS I WANT TO ACHIEVE

1

2

3

4

5

6

7

8

9

10

THE MOST MEANINGFUL THING THAT HAPPENED TODAY...

DAY ....

DAY ....

DAY ....

DAY ....

THE MOST MEANINGFUL THING THAT HAPPENED TODAY...

DAY _____

_____

_____

_____

_____

DAY _____

_____

_____

_____

_____

DAY _____

_____

_____

_____

_____

DAY _____

_____

_____

_____

_____

THE MOST MEANINGFUL THING THAT HAPPENED TODAY...

DAY ......

DAY ......

DAY ......

DAY ......

LOOK BACK OVER
THE PREVIOUS PAGES
TOP 10 SENTENCES
IN MY JOURNAL

1

2

3

4

5

6

7

8

9

10

The most meaningful thing that happened today...

Day ....

Day ....

Day ....

Day ....

THE MOST MEANINGFUL THING THAT HAPPENED TODAY...

DAY ......

DAY ......

DAY ......

DAY ......

THE MOST MEANINGFUL THING THAT HAPPENED TODAY...

DAY___

DAY ___

DAY ___

DAY ___

THE MOST MEANINGFUL THING THAT HAPPENED TODAY...

DAY ......

DAY ......

DAY ......

DAY ......

The most meaningful thing that happened today...

Day ....

Day ....

Day | ....

Day | ....

THE MOST MEANINGFUL...

BOOK:

FILM:

SONG:

PERSON:

MEAL:

EVENT:

WALK:

TRIP:

HOLIDAY:

ADVENTURE:

CONVERSATION:

ACHIEVEMENT:

DAY:

REALISATION:

PRESENT:

THING THAT I HAVE DONE FOR SOMEONE:

THING THAT SOMEONE HAS DONE FOR ME:

THE BEST SENTENCE IN MY JOURNAL

DESCRIBE WHY:

COLLECT & STICK IN MEANINGFUL MEMORIES:

COLLECT & STICK IN MEANINGFUL MEMORIES:

COLLECT & STICK IN MEANINGFUL MEMORIES:

PUBLISHING DIRECTOR Sarah Lavelle
EDITOR Romilly Morgan
CREATIVE DIRECTOR Helen Lewis
DESIGNER Emily Lapworth
COVER ARTWORK Katie Horwich
PRODUCTION DIRECTOR Vincent Smith
PRODUCTION CONTROLLER Emily Noto

First published in 2015 by
Quadrille Publishing Ltd
Pentagon House
52-54 Southwark Street
London SE1 1UN
www.quadrille.co.uk

Compilation, design and
layout © 2015 Quadrille
Publishing

Cover artwork
© 2015 Katie Horwich

Cover map
© Map Resources

Quadrille is an imprint
of Hardie Grant
www.hardiegrant.com.au

The publisher has made
every effort to trace the
copyright holders. We
apologise in advance for
any unintentional omissions
and would be pleased to
insert the appropriate
acknowledgement in any
subsequent edition.

British Library Cataloguing-
in-Publication Data
A catalogue record for this
book is available from the
British Library.

ISBN: 978 184949 741 1

Printed in China